1100
architect

1100
architect

Essay by Donald Albrecht

THE MONACELLI PRESS

Library of Congress Cataloging-in-Publication Data
1100 Architect / essay by Donald Albrecht.
p.   cm.
ISBN 1-58093-178-2
1. 1100 Architect (Firm)–Themes, motives. 2. Architecture–New York (State)–
New York–20th century. 3. Architecture–New York (State)–New York–21st century.
I. Albrecht, Donald. II. Title: Eleven Hundred Architect.
NA737.A16A4   2006
720.92'2–dc22   2006015956

Printed and bound in China

Designed by Abbott Miller and Christine Moog, Pentagram

Cover: Watermill Houses, Watermill, New York, 2003;
photograph by Peter Aaron, ESTO

CONTENTS

AN ARCHITECTURE OF TRANSPARENCY
Donald Albrecht

A series of iconic images defines the work of 1100 Architect and suggests the qualities that distinguish its projects. A limestone-clad Manhattan townhouse that opens up inside to a four-story skylit floating stair obscured by a screen of translucent metal mesh. A laboratory/gallery for a cosmetics company with walls and fixtures of skinlike translucency. A museum shop where artifacts float in and out behind theatrical scrims. An Okinawa apartment house and gallery with shojilike glass walls of varying degrees of transparency. A progressive elementary school in New York City where children learn social activism in an environment strongly connected to its urban setting.

While functionally and architecturally diverse, these projects are linked by common themes, best described by terms outside of traditional design vocabulary, such as transparency, fluidity, and permeability. Since the firm's establishment in 1983, partners David Piscuskas and Juergen Riehm have sought to design buildings and interiors in an "apparently transparent style." Even the firm's name, derived from the suite number on the door of its first New York office, suggests 1100's commitment to crossing thresholds and maintaining a design sensibility responsive to many forces. The intention is to transcend perceived boundaries—physical, cultural, and metaphorical— to create buildings and interiors that are open to individual interpretation. "A recognizable form," the architects note, "invites the individual to distinguish it through personal association."

1100's search for a transparent style that goes beyond dogma and fashion has been a rallying cry shared with such contemporaries as architects Steven Harris and Deborah Berke as well as a stabilizing aspiration in the turbulence of recent architectural -isms. Forming their partnership at the height of postmodernism—Philip Johnson's AT&T Building was completed the following year—Piscuskas and Riehm assiduously resisted the style's overt historicist pastiche, also steering clear of the parade of formalist styles that followed in its wake. Instead, they seek to address modern needs and tastes by expanding upon the spatial, structural, and material innovations of modernism's first generation—not only its masters like Le Corbusier but also lesser-known figures like Adolf Loos and William Lescaze. 1100's astylar spaces are often enriched by a luxurious use of sensuous materials—both modern substances like glass and plastic that obscure, reveal, and distort and also time-honored materials that firmly situate the architects' work within the history of architecture and design. For instance, Loos selected black marble and onyx in his American Bar (1908) in Vienna, updating these ancient materials with a grid setting. Following his lead, 1100 Architect uses brown suede and Venetian plaster for planar walls, figured woods for streamlined handrails, and massive rough-hewn stones for utilitarian washbasins, all detailed in a distinctly contemporary fashion.

The firm's interest in transcending boundaries is manifested in a variety of architectural strategies. 1100 frequently uses different kinds of glass to create a permeable interface between interior and exterior. While its Watermill Houses compound (2003), on a wooded Long Island site, looks back to advances in glass architecture in Ludwig Mies van der Rohe's Farnsworth House (1951) outside Chicago and Philip Johnson's Glass House (1949) in New Canaan, Connecticut, a group of recent urban projects employs new and innovative technologies. 1100 explores the surprising potential of the substance in New York's Plotkin Residence (2005), where an eerily dematerialized stairway of cantilevered, frosted-glass treads leads to a rooftop den and exterior terrace separated from each other by a thirty-six-foot-long wall of glass curving in multiple directions like a wave of water. Here, 1100 combines the modernist interest in glass as a transparent material with more recent innovations that allow glass to be treated as a sculptural material. From the den, the glass wall offers spectacular city views, while from the terrace the wavy glass provides a distorted, fun-house view of the same cityscape.

In the Naha City Gallery and Apartment House (2003) in Okinawa Prefecture, Japan, 1100 Architect created a building where transparent and solid, permeable and impermeable, intersect to form a clear diagram of the building's program.

In order to shield the building's interiors from neighbors on adjacent lots, the structure's east and west facades are made of mirror-smooth concrete punctuated by small windows; the windows form pinpoints of natural light in the buildings' stairways. In contrast, the north and south facades are fully glazed with three different kinds of glass to flood the living and retail spaces with natural light and offer views of a nearby park. The various types of glass express the diverse program: transparent glass sheathes the building's gallery and retail spaces and the apartments' living and dining rooms; alternating panes of translucent and opaque glass afford privacy to the apartments' bedrooms and bathrooms. 1100 Architect further defines the building's public versus private functions by locating the gallery and retail spaces on a tall *piano nobile* that cantilevers over the ground-floor garage. Naha's limited and muted material palette, typical of much of 1100's work, continues to the interior, which features exposed polished concrete ceilings, dark walnut floors, and walls of lighter sycamore panels. The building's wood, concrete, and glass surfaces are all subdivided into precise grids— a strategy that unifies interior and exterior.

Though more modest than many of their commissions, 1100's renovation and expansion of Greenwich Village's Little Red School House and Elisabeth Irwin High School (1999 and 2002) demonstrates a modernist strategy of open interior spaces and permeable edges where city and institution intersect. Founded in the 1920s by progressive educator Elisabeth Irwin, this independent school for more than five hundred students fosters an open pedagogy of self-motivated learning and social activism. By the mid-1990s, as enrollment expanded, the school needed to grow beyond its cramped quarters of two existing buildings. 1100's thoughtful design links these historic structures, not only creating a unified forty-two-thousand-square-foot campus, which students now easily traverse throughout the day, but also reorienting the school's primary entrance from a narrow side street to a landscaped plaza on Sixth Avenue. Fronting on this plaza, the new red-brick-clad structure houses light-filled classrooms and art studios as well as communal spaces:

cafeteria, gymnasium, and glass-walled library. Located on street level to signify the institution's educational mission, the library is set back from Sixth Avenue and raised a few feet above the sidewalk. This simple gesture offers students within both visual connectivity to and contemplative distance from the dynamic city outside. This strategy also allowed the insertion, beneath the raised library floor, of a clerestory window that brings natural light into the lower-level cafeteria. There, an undulating ceiling of wooden slats—one of many homages to Alvar Aalto that populate 1100's work—carries reflected light deep into the underground space and creates a memorable element that students encounter daily.

The Little Red School House demonstrates 1100 Architect's commitment to creating well-conceived and orderly plans that combine traditional ideas of discrete rooms with open planning concepts of modernists like Mies and Le Corbusier, bringing natural light and spatial fluidity into otherwise dark and claustrophobic Manhattan buildings. For the firm's residential clients, many of 1100's urban projects follow in the footsteps of architects like John Soane and Paul Rudolph, whose own townhouses featured staid exteriors that served to heighten open interiors. The juxtaposition of the expected and the unexpected gives these buildings their dramatic power.

1100's design of a new twelve-thousand-square-foot, four-story townhouse on Manhattan's Upper East Side (2005) updates this tradition. An austere front facade interprets the white stucco of William Lescaze's own New York townhouse in more durable limestone panels and floor-to-ceiling windows in thin metal frames. The house's upper three floors are pressed tight to the lot line and cantilever over the ground floor, creating a recessed entrance. This sober exterior makes the interior all the more striking. Visitors, entering through solid wood doors into a small, double-height foyer, are met by another barrier, a translucent wall of metal mesh, through which a full-height stairway cantilevered twenty-five feet from a central wall seductively beckons. Like many of the architects' custom-designed stairways, this one twists and turns in faceted forms that are illuminated from a skylight above. Referencing Louis I. Kahn's dictum that architects should never design standard elements as if they came out of a catalog, 1100 Architect treats the stair as an art piece, cladding it in exotic black-and-gray-veined wenge and highlighting it with custom-designed, Art Deco–inspired metal balustrades. This stair serves as the organizing device around which the house's spaces unfold. The effect is a visual dialogue between the restless and the calm, the sculptural and the spatial. The stair provides a counterpoint to the serene, interconnected arrangements of comfortable spaces around it, which are graciously linked to one another via broad openings and sliding doors and combine loftlike openness with the privacy and intimacy of traditional rooms.

The interiors of the Upper East Side townhouse suggest another distinctive facet of 1100's work: their astylar spaces often serve as showcases for collections—contemporary art, African artifacts, mid-twentieth-century design, vintage fashion—that represent their clients' passions and personalities. While the townhouse's mix of living room chairs inspired by Hollywood decorator Billy Haines, crystal-chandeliered bathtubs, and custom-designed carpets defines the high end of domestic interior design today, other residential projects initiate a dialogue between artifact and architecture that amplifies viewers' perceptions of clients' collections. In a penthouse renovation on Manhattan's East Side (2002), 1100 Architect worked with interior designer Tony Ingrao to develop a design language of geometric forms that complements the abstract shapes of paintings by Victor Vasarely and Bridget Riley. Glass portholes in the apartment's interior doors, a rounded conversation pit in the living room, a circular dining table by Eero Saarinen, and pillows upholstered in graphic black-and-white fabrics by Verner Panton link interior design and artwork. In a duplex in New York (2002), 1100 Architect provides a subtle backdrop that takes its cues from the client's collection of minimalist stainless-steel furniture by Danish master Poul Kjaerholm, setting it against an equally simple interior of built-in cabinetry with flush details, recessed lighting, and stainless-steel handrails.

Similarly, 1100's commercial projects often function as theatrical showcases for objects for sale. For New York's Museum of Modern Art, which commissioned two design stores (1999 and 2001), the architects developed a system of translucent screens—luminous scrims that alternate between concealing and revealing products—to dramatize and transform shoppers' perceptions of objects. The double-height store across from the museum on West Fifty-third Street includes mezzanine-level display vitrines in which modern furnishings by such designers as Charles and Ray Eames and Philippe Starck seemingly float behind scrims of metal mesh. They are at times illuminated, at times darkened, by computerized theater lighting. MoMA's Soho store features a backlit polyvinyl membrane that connects the store's two floors into a seamless environment that both sells and celebrates contemporary design. The design was partly inspired, says lighting consultant Bill Schwinghammer, by a 1950s George Nelson bubble lamp. Shining through large plate-glass windows, this bold white lighting converts the store's historic cast-iron space into a bright beacon. It is less austere, and more accessible, than MoMA's galleries, but it is a stunning vitrine for objets d'art nevertheless.

1100's work for the Japanese cosmetics and fragrance company Shiseido demonstrates another strategy of transparency and translucency that is used to spotlight commercial goods. In Shiseido's gallery/laboratories, one in New York City (1999) and one in Santa Monica, California (2000), 1100 has designed an ephemeral environment that evokes the company's own sensuously packaged products. Angled or curved walls, counters, and display tables subtly modulate the long, rectangular rooms of both studios into flowing, irregular spatial sequences. Walls are both solid plaster and translucent glass. Some are backlit with brightly colored strips of light; others feature indirectly lit niches for the artful display of products. Countertops are finished in smooth molded resin. Walls magically disappear into indirectly lit ceiling coves, and counters float on illuminated reveals to achieve a Zenlike atmosphere that is both luxurious and ascetic. In many ways, the Shiseido studios are updated versions of the spaces created in the 1930s by Jean-Michel Frank; the Frenchman's motto for his own work applies to 1100's as well: "one doesn't work in centimeters, but in millimeters."

In twenty-five years of projects, from townhouses to stores and apartment interiors, 1100's work has demonstrated an enduring commitment to the creation of commodious spaces with well-conceived and orderly plans, elegant proportions, fine materials, exacting details, and bountiful light. But perhaps the aspect of 1100's work that distinguishes it most from that of other architects is its exploration of those qualities of architecture that can be intuitively experienced and that can accommodate varied ways of occupying it. In its pursuit, the architects acknowledge a debt to Mies van der Rohe, whose open-ended aesthetic serves as a philosophical touchstone. At the same time, objects play an important role in 1100's search for this architecture of transparency. Whether designing for Eames chairs, skin-care products, or Vasarely canvases, 1100 Architect creates a shared visual language for each project that sparks a dialogue between artifact and architecture, leaving room, according to Piscuskas and Riehm, for interpretation and discussion as well as for memories and desires.

TERMS AND CONDITIONS

JUERGEN RIEHM We started the firm with the idea of a collaborative effort. In the early days, we worked mostly with artists, and what we had was a dialogue, a give and take. This type of involvement and discourse created a precedent for us as a firm.

DAVID PISCUSKAS And our ethos has not changed drastically—it is a natural and intuitive act that we perform. But as an architect or an office becomes better known, there is an expectation that the vision will be more defined, more coherent and fixed.

JR For us, it is crucial that we *not* have a fixed point of view. There is an expectation that we have a vision, and we do; but we don't have a *preconceived* vision. We don't say, "Here's a sketch. This is going to be your house. I did it on the airplane!" Life is not made that way. It is important to be accepting of the human condition, the variables and the choices. That's why we quite often ask, What does this building want to be ultimately? And we keep pushing the design through this type of inquiry and exploration. It is not a formula that we are going to crank out.

DP Each project has specific terms and conditions that make it unique. As the design evolves, we begin to perceive a sense of what it is—how hard it is versus how soft it is, how light it is versus how dark it is. If it becomes too strident in any direction, we adjust the balance, readdress that component. We attempt to join process and aesthetic.

JR Every commission is a new experience for us as well as for the client—each project is alive and active. Architecture endeavors to create spaces that can be experienced; when the experience is open and free for interpretation, ownership is offered to anyone who inhabits it.

DP Allowing for this type of openness means not subscribing to a theory or an -ism. When there isn't an -ism, a label, there's often the perception that the design solution has not been derived from a thoughtful process. In fact, there is more deliberation and more sincerity in a process that has not been systematized or labeled.

JR While we avoid labels or excessive theorizing, we are very inclusive in terms of what we seek. There has to be an aim, an *ultimus*, to expand our way of thinking.

DP Inclusive does not mean that anything and everything goes when it comes to designing a building, or that we don't make judgments. There is inclusivity in recognizing that there are a number of ways in which things can be done. What we consistently do is give our clients a more inclusive knowledge of architectural possibilities. Because in every instance of good, well-conceived architecture, you have a client who is informed and involved in the process.

JR This means sharing and engaging the client. It requires a certain internal attitude to be able to give a lot during a project and then to be able to walk away and be satisfied with the fact that presumably your client is enjoying what you gave them—the client now owns the experience.

DP It's a difficult task to try to find something that is ineffable and speaks to an individual and collective unconscious. We believe most people, ourselves included, want to connect with their neighbors and friends, with the time in which they are living; by extension, they want to have created or participated in something that lives on.

JR This ties into "desire," which is something we often talk about: the client's desire, our own desires, a larger desire for society and the environment, and also the desire to carry your ideas through to the tiniest details. Desire is a motivator, an initiator, a motor.

DP Ideally, our desires for an architectural space can be made possible through the built environment. This isn't to say that the "paper architecture" or "screen architecture" aspect of what we do has no relevance, because it does. But there are pragmatic conditions that arise when you try to realize these ideas and desires in built form.

JR The effect of these pragmatic conditions on a design is exemplified by the materiality of the design: the characteristics of a material are related not only to its durability and its simple visual attributes but to its qualities of sensuousness and tactility. But materials must also be grounded and employed with purpose, and a consideration of how they will transform themselves over time is crucial.

DP There's another aspect of materiality that recurs in our thinking: we do not announce or make a statement about how materials are fastened. This becomes important in creating clarity and seductiveness; it immediately introduces the viewer to the whole of the space.

JR Concealment is also about restraint, so that a space becomes self-effacing and discreet, not showy or talking too much about itself.

DP The painter Chuck Close begins with a very literal image, but there is a process by which that literal image is rendered that is very complex; he labors over each unit of color in the grid. He makes decisions and then constantly goes back and reevaluates. This parallels our process—turning from the literal to the abstract and back again, telescoping and microscoping until a project is fully realized.

JR As with painting, or other art forms, there are conditions we are dealing with, ingredients at our disposal. We contemplate how we want a project to feel and what might be an appropriate gesture for each element. It is fairly complex how the architectural space manifests. Conditions that are outside of your control often become moments for improvisation and creativity—that is, if you are poised, engaged in the world, and ready to use the world's fabric and context as impetus. What is achieved through this process is, we hope, gestalt—an essence that transcends the conception of a work at both telescopic and microscopic scales.

DP For an architect to engage all of these pragmatic and holistic levels, he or she needs to be optimistic. We're constantly writing the rules we think apply to a project and then looking to break them or adjust them: we are improvising to a certain degree. This might mean a new direction or a specific reality that finds its way into the process. Our firm's name is something of an example. 1100 is a sign, a symbol; it's an abstraction, it could be a binary code. The one and the zero are very abstract numbers. But 1100 is literal: it is a very real, very small place, the address of our first office. So the contrast of the extreme pragmatism and the coincidence/serendipity of that locale turned into an abstract name that we have kept.

JR Since our firm's inception in Suite 1100 at 225 Lafayette Street, we have continually grown and evolved. We are still discovering new things, but we do not forget what we have experienced, or what philosophers have written. Nor do we feel the need to get every idea we have into a project—our decisions aren't arbitrary. Ultimately, there is a kernel to be realized in each project, and that kernel informs the process and guides our ideas.

DP And there is kinetic energy that we are trying to preserve, not exhaust. We continually ask ourselves, How do you absorb something— a problem, a raw fact, that kernel of an idea—and elevate it or abstract it to expose its meaning?

This dialogue represents conversations between David Piscuskas and Juergen Riehm, moderated by Ines Elskop, in New York, in February and March 2006.

PROJECTS

ABELL RESIDENCE

New York, New York, 1998

This duplex in lower Manhattan integrates two distinctly separate floors into one coherent space. An expressively carved central vortex of staircase and light well celebrates and unifies the apartment spatially even as the insertion affects a boundary between public and private. The staircase also expresses the owner's affinity for adventure and the outdoors, its organic geometry recalling the water-carved rock passages he has experienced in his travels. The association with the natural environment is refined in the master suite. Crisp rolled-steel and glass panels permit varying degrees of openness or separation between the sleeping and bathing domains. The materials in the residence – honed bluestone, rift-sawn oak, carved limestone, polished mahogany – extend the deference to the natural; yet the brightly colored acrylic panels of the kitchen and the crushed, tempered glass embedded in the polished concrete floor evidence the processed existence of urban life.

The client's predilection for the grand Baroque staircases of seventeenth- and eighteenth-century Europe inspired an elliptical intervention; as a spatial strategy, it enhances the scale and open quality of the two levels of the apartment.

LITTLE RED SCHOOL HOUSE AND
ELISABETH IRWIN HIGH SCHOOL

New York, New York, 1999, 2002

A series of distinct projects at the Little Red School House and Elisabeth Irwin High School, a progressive independent school, aspires to transform the perception of the school from within, and also throughout the larger community of lower Manhattan. By integrating fifteen thousand square feet of new space and fully renovating the existing facilities, the design develops communal learning spaces and social environments and reconceives the way the buildings are used.

The most significant and visible aspect is a new structure at Little Red, which occupies a small parcel abutted on two sides by existing school facilities; it contains a new library linked to a technology classroom, two additional classrooms, a cafeteria, and mechanical and heating plants. The library is emphasized literally and figuratively by its visibility and location: it is adjacent to the entrance and is accessible from the park outside. On the third floor, a middle-school art studio with a thirteen-foot peaked skylight replaces the former basement-level classroom. A new entry plaza on Avenue of the Americas increases the visibility of the school in the community, makes available a better meeting point for parents and children, and maximizes daylight for the new spaces. A subsequent addition to the building provides a lower-school gymnasium and middle-school science laboratory.

The main entrance to the school was transposed from an unwieldy location on Bleecker Street to a more spacious and functional entry plaza fronting an existing park on Avenue of the Americas now known as "Little Red Square."

The interplay between a thin ribbon of natural light, coaxed from under the platform of the library above, and a suspended undulating surface, comprised of 275 battens of white Georgia ash, brings character and warmth to the cafeteria ceiling.

The middle-school studio emphasizes the importance of the fine arts and arts education for both the school and the local community. Occupying a prominent space at the front of the new building, the classroom has large studio windows and oblique skylights that funnel daylight into the space.

MoMA DESIGN STORE, MIDTOWN

New York, New York, 1999

The design store for the Museum of Modern Art, located in midtown Manhattan, reinforces the institution's identity as a platform for modern and contemporary art. The parti creates a space with innovative and functional displays of furniture, design objects, books, and accessories. The entrance, in the west corner, immediately offers visitors a sweeping view of the store. Material, light, and color usher movement through the showroom, presenting merchandise in a logical visual progression. The east wall of the store is faceted with a floor-to-ceiling grid, backlit with diffused neon lighting, of adjustable vertical and horizontal shelves; the softly glowing matrix brings out the clean lines of contemporary furniture. A virtual mezzanine – a steel-mesh encasement – increases the sales area. Computerized theater lighting, lit from the foreground or from behind the steel scrim, spotlights individual pieces. The composition of light through scrim allows for wholly different views of the space and lends depth to an otherwise hidden area.

A luminous material palette, including European beech paneling and anodized aluminum shelving, offsets the saturated colors of the merchandise. Undulating walls with sandblasted acrylic shelving provide additional display space. Niche tableaus draw attention to smaller design objects, while islands of neon-irradiated plastic-laminate cabinetry exhibit additional merchandise. A cobalt blue rubberized floor, which yields underfoot, balances the light-colored materials.

Neon tubing – more than 260 feet of it – was
deployed throughout the store. Slipped into a notch
at the back of the curvilinear shelves, the tubes
limn the display surface.

Neon strips inserted into the upright supports of
the full-height gridded display reflect a lustrous field
of light off the white walls for a diffuse glow and
dematerializing effect. Such plays of concealment
and revelation distinguish details throughout
the store.

SHAHID & COMPANY

New York, New York, 1999

Advertising agency Shahid & Company requested an elegant and functional office. Equally important was a work environment that was unrestricted – to support the generation of creativity and ideas – but with the capacity to hold private meetings for clients and company management. A studio space segmented by freestanding partitions offers both public and private areas. In contrast to the fluid and expressive spatial quality of the plan, materials are limited to gypsum wall board, plywood, and steel, fostering a serene and refined office space that reflects the image of the client.

Only four low partitions segment the entirety of the
six-thousand-square-foot studio space, opening vistas
through and across the office and fostering a sense
of community among the employees. Practical
elements – lighting fixtures, ventilation ducts –
reference the original architecture of the loft space;
materials and furnishings instead propose a contrast.

SHISEIDO STUDIOS

New York, New York, 1999
Santa Monica, California, 2000

Intended to introduce the philosophy and products of the cosmetics company, the Shiseido Studios function predominantly as gallery and clinic rather than as commercial space. Designed as series of unfolding planes and connected spaces, with faintly hued glass partitions, bleached wood, and concrete floors speckled with tan and gray, the studios feel clean and unobtrusive yet engage the senses. Smooth, molded resin countertops and fabric-lined walls create tactile surfaces that conspire with gentle lighting to provide a warm ambience. The lighting is indirect, entering through a trough in the ceiling and reflecting off the walls or filtering through layers of translucent acrylic. Studio details – steel merchandise trays and glass cabinets – give prominence to the small sculptural forms of the Shiseido line and heighten the sensory experience of the visit.

Within the single conceptual model that characterizes both studios, variations evidence sensitivity to location and environmental conditions. Santa Monica's temperate climate suggested an open studio with many points of entry and an incorporation of the exterior; natural light bathes the space from all directions. In New York's Soho, a floor-through layout allows only one entry and therefore implies a linear narration of space. An LED light panel on the back wall changes colors throughout the day, softly illuminating product displays.

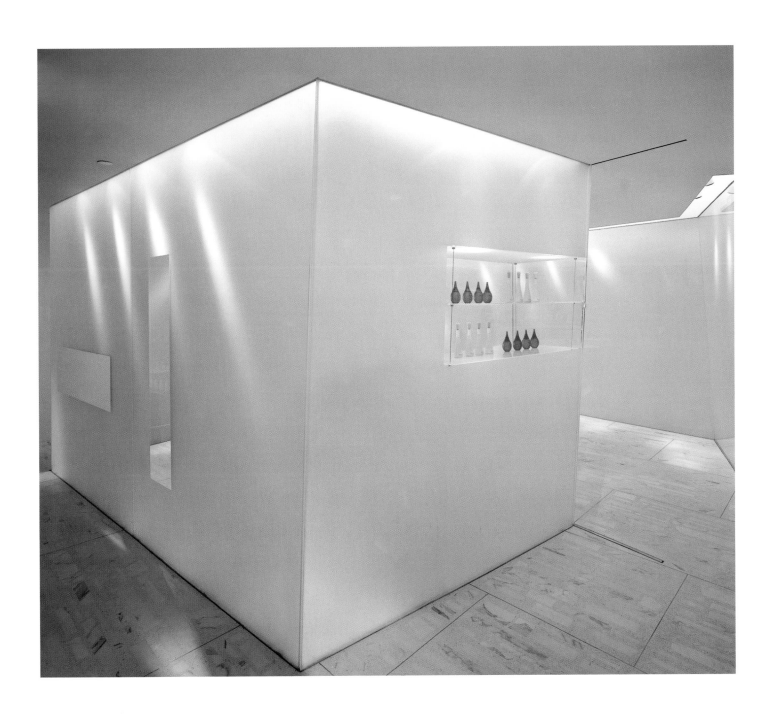

shiseido studio

WEST VILLAGE TOWNHOUSE
New York, New York, 2000

This four-thousand-square-foot townhouse, originally constructed in the mid-1800s, is one of the row of houses that once stood close to the banks of the Hudson River. The house required comprehensive reconstruction subject to the approval of the Landmarks Preservation Commission. Another aim of the renovation was to open up an extension on the rear facade affixed many years after completion of the historic building and isolated by the massive entry wall.

Underlying the reconfiguration was the incorporation of new materials and details, the juxtaposition of past and present, and the maximization of paths for natural light. Skylights and glass floor panels allow light to penetrate vertically through the house. The rear facade was effectively dematerialized to form a two-story glass-walled garden room that introduces daylight to both the basement dining room and the first-floor kitchen; it integrates glass and steel with the brick arches of the original house. Concurrence of new and old infrastructures is even more apparent in the interior, where exposed steel beams and curved plaster walls are coupled with antique wood floor joists and exposed brick walls.

HOLBROOK RESIDENCE
New York, New York, 2000

This former taxi garage in downtown Manhattan has been transformed into a spacious five-level home with a patio and rooftop garden. It was important to carefully redeploy all of the space in the building, a previously enlarged and rather haphazard array of accretions. While the structural system remained unchanged, the floor plates were reconfigured, carved to form an illuminated incision within the core of the house. This delineation is accented by the twisting spine of the central stair.

Designing an environment for the client's large collection of African art and objects was an equally vital component of the renovation. Interior spaces juxtapose light and dark to contrast with and accentuate the earth tones of the pieces. The first two floors consist of airy living and dining spaces. The third level, an open mezzanine, exploits the fourth-floor skylight, distributing natural light throughout the house. Enhancing the openness of the design, the sunlight exhibits the art in a way that recalls its natural environment.

The forms of Dogon, Senoufo, Bamun, and Fang carved-wood artifacts, all from West Africa, inspired the central staircase/light well and other sectional cuts through the building.

BONNIE'S K9

New York, New York, 2000

German shepherd Bonnie was the paradigmatic user and model for this canine health center. Confined to a cage for the first months of her life, Bonnie was nurtured to mobility through an extensive program of hydrotherapy. This experience inspired her owner to offer similar resources to other animals. Bonnie's K9 combines a holistic dog-food preparation facility and a veterinarian's office into a 1,500-square-foot rehabilitation center with garden, pool, and boarding cabins in the shell of a former meatpacking plant in West Chelsea. Durable yet refined materials including high-density fiber-cement sheets and anodized aluminum create a fresh and serene atmosphere. In the swim center, a stretched Barrisol membrane ceiling suspended on curved aluminum rails and clear-cedar-plank and aluminum benches suggest spa rather than kennel. A fifteen-by-ten-foot pool captures reflections of the lush rear garden.

Bonnie's K9 Corp.

Naturally Raw

Animal Natural
Healing Center

9

EFFORTLESSNESS An action that appears eff

A good designer necessarily expends effort: disci

and edits the myriad impulses that accompar

a straightforward, elegant, and meaningful de

architecture inspires ease in the viewer: it is

meeting visual or sensory distraction. A reduc

well-balanced proportions, and careful detailir

architectural space. Is there any other relations

that of effortlessness? We have always question

an *effect* of effortlessness: work that resoun

designer's hand is almost invisible.

ess is seldom the result of an effortless process.
ed and lateral minded, he or she both entertains
project, honing only the foremost of these into
. There is no margin for error. Well-designed
acute pleasure to inhabit a structure without
hough scrupulously selected material palette,
ree the viewer to absorb the serenity of an
of cause and effect so riddled with paradox as
how even to evoke it. We aspire at least toward
vith a sense of clarity, with a sense that the

MoMA DESIGN STORE, SOHO
New York, New York, 2001

The MoMA Design Store, Soho, located on Spring Street, is the second commercial extension of the Museum of Modern Art. The project converts two floors of a warehouse building – a historic landmark—into a space for transitory yet seamless displays of furniture, design objects, and books.

The design, which emphasizes light and suppleness, maintains certain of the structural elements of the original warehouse. Abutting the open stairwell is a double-height surface of exposed brick. Antique cast-iron columns are enveloped in faceted, sandblasted glass panels. Fiber-optic lighting illuminates the columns from within, lending a radiant quality to the crystalline encasements. The two levels of the showroom are unified by a translucent Barrisol membrane covering the ceiling and walls in a continuous curve. Lit from behind, the plane illuminates the interior with a diffused glow. Two forms of lighting highlight the products – soft ambient light of fluorescent tubes and cool neon – adding a sense of depth to the displays. Modular floor cabinets, mounted on plinths, allow the showroom to be easily and quickly rearranged to suit the ever-changing merchandise.

Typically, retail design demands focused accent lighting. At this store for furniture and design objects, a unified light source – 282 fluorescent strips – illuminates the entire showroom in a seamless wash.

A silver-gray glaze neutralizes the variegated maple floor, which is original to this historic warehouse building. The gridded furniture display recalls the aluminum wall fixtures of MoMA's midtown store.

IRISH HUNGER MEMORIAL

New York, New York, 2002

Sponsored by the Hugh L. Carey Battery Park City Authority, the Irish Hunger Memorial commemorates the great Irish hunger and migration of 1845–50. A contemplative space where visitors explore the famine and its connections to world hunger today, the memorial ultimately aims to effect social change. The design, winner of an invited competition, was developed by artist Brian Tolle, landscape architect Gail Eileen Wittwer, and 1100 Architect.

The memorial re-creates a rugged Irish landscape atop a modern base to generate an experiential reflection on the famine. A ruined famine-era cottage from County Mayo, donated to the project by the Slack family, is accessed from two paths, one that meanders across the landscape and another that connects diagonally through the base. This roofless structure recalls the desperate farmers who tore the thatch off their homes to prove destitution, thereby qualifying for famine relief. The landscape surrounding the cottage resembles abandoned fields and overgrown potato furrows. Also included in the memorial are stones gathered from each of Ireland's thirty-two counties.

The base for the landscape is an illuminated stone and glass structure that rises from street level at the southeastern corner to a height of twenty-five feet at the western end. The highest point of the cantilevered landscape offers views of the Hudson River, the Statue of Liberty, and Ellis Island, connecting the memorial to nearby landmarks. The base is inscribed with texts drawn from varied sources – parliamentary reports to recipes – that recount the history of the Irish hunger alongside stories of other world hunger issues past and present.

Honed, fossilized Irish limestone in the base
structure and cantilevered landscape references
the layers of history surrounding the events of
the great hunger. Cleft-surfaced pavers flank the
sidewalk, connecting the memorial tangibly with
the present.

It was vital to materialize the text of this living
memorial. Quotations are printed rather than
inscribed onto panels enclosed behind glass;
the panels are considered unfinished and the
text may be updated at any time.

GOVERNMENT SOUP: 100 GALLONS OF WATER,

IN THE EVENT OF UNEMPLOYMENT, SICKNESS, DISABILITY, WIDOWHOOD OR OLD

2 1/2 POUNDS OF BEEF, 6 1/2 POUNDS OF DRIPPINGS, 13 POUNDS OF

TO SHARE HIS SCANTY MEAL WITH HIS STARVING NEIGHBOR

AR SCÁTH A CHÉILE A MHAIREANN NA DAOINE. PEOPLE LIVE IN ONE ANOTHER'S SHELTER.

FAMINE POLICY TAKES TIME.

WE ARE STRUGGLING TO KEEP ON OUR BREAKFASTS AS THE ONLY MEANS [THE CHILDREN HAVE] AND TO CLOTHE THE DESTITUTE

1849: 214,425. 1850: 9,054. 1851: 249,721.

MANHATTAN DUPLEX

New York, New York, 2002

Lighting and luxurious materials combine in this rich yet simple living space on two floors of a prewar building. While the original layout of the duplex remains relatively unchanged, this new manifestation addresses the needs and desires of contemporary living in an essay on natural and artificial light. By day, generous arrays of windows fill the living spaces with abundant sunlight. By night, artificial light, discreetly sourced, achieves a comparable glow. Ribbons of light both define and smooth interior edges, causing wall, ceiling, and floor planes to visually dissolve. Fittings such as a wall of floor-to-ceiling cabinets that traverses living room and kitchen unify the residence while respecting the independent character of each room. The concealed light fixtures and absence of hardware contribute to the minimalist character, as do the seemingly paper-thin white walls.

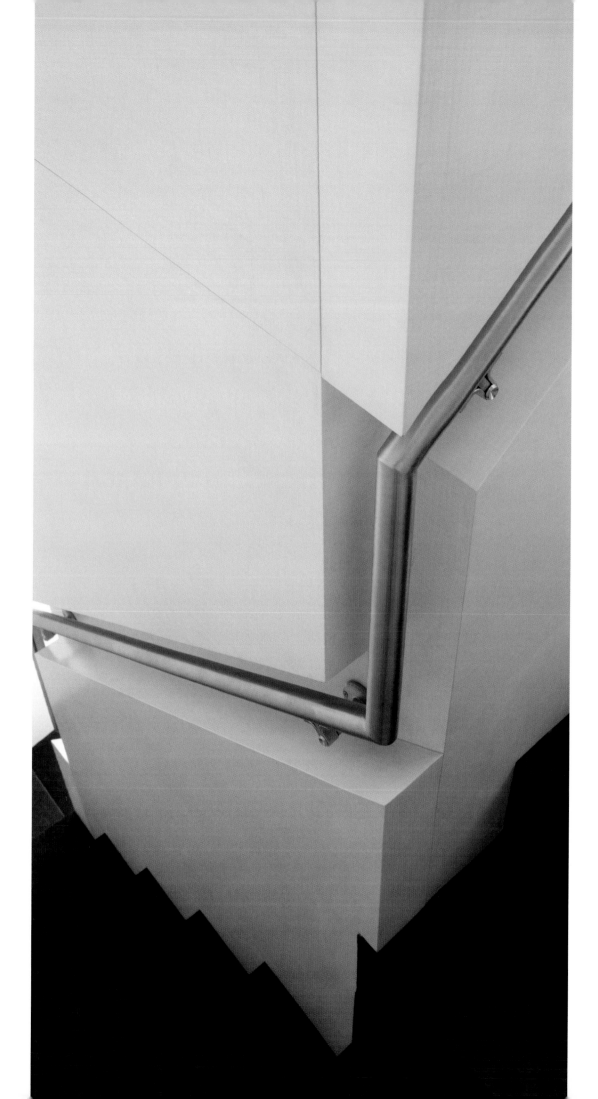

MATERIALITY Materials are imbued with r

recognition, significantly shaping the experience

of a material – whether it is supple, brittle, trans

it is manipulated evoke presence and absenc

fundamental to the vocabulary of architecture.

words to convey a certain meaning, there is po

bring into being a certain place. Materials may h

be raw, finished, decomposed, or fabricated. Te

endless signification: plastic endowed with sele

by fluidity and impermanence. Our work reflec

places of self-production and self-reflection.

hing. They elicit memory, desire, agitation, and

architectural space. The sensory characteristics

nt, cool, elastic, crude – and the extent to which

eight and density, light and time. Materiality is

as there is poetry in selecting a specific word or

in choosing a specific material or materials to

fixed qualities within mutable states: they may

ology amplifies mutability, creating a culture of

tributes of glass; corrugated metal differentiated

urposeful, honest material choices, giving rise to

EAST SIDE PENTHOUSE

New York, New York, 2002

The unusual site for this penthouse consisted of a quirky composition of interconnected roof structures atop a turn-of-the-century apartment building on the banks of the East River in Manhattan. The amalgam required fundamental changes in planning and structure to function as a modern residence. The clients' personal style and sensibilities – emphatically modern – as well as their extensive art collection were critical in developing an architectural expression that is at once unique and livable.

Significant portions of the various preexisting components were reconfigured to create an avenue of circulation along the apartment's outermost edges. The form of this pathway, while itself delimited by the architecture, shapes the coherent and recognizable plan for the domestic functions of the penthouse. The circumferential route offers dramatic views of the river nearby and the city beyond, yet it is also a self-sufficient element of architecture with furrowed planes and concealed lighting.

In the living spaces demarcated by the circulation avenue, walls arc into ceilings, blurring boundaries and creating continuous, infinite spaces. Narrow hallways open into large foyers and rooms, and a spacious kitchen occupies the center of the apartment. The palette of materials in the luminous, sculpted spaces is spare and not conventionally luxurious: marble-based epoxy, stainless and hot-rolled steel, plaster, acrylic, and painted wood.

Nestled within a three-quarter-inch crevice in the
walls of the gallery is a thin tube of white neon.
This concealed fixture highlights the surface of the
uppermost curve; variations on this treatment recur
throughout the apartment.

A dense array of neon tubes behind a sheet of frosted
Plexiglas at the back of the bookshelves illuminates
the library, sculpting each volume in light.

121

Maximum occupancy of the capacious kitchen is fifty-eight. This spiritual center of the home is also the physical center, with pathways to both private and public domains.

FASHIONHAUS

New York, New York, 2003

Housed in a converted warehouse building in midtown Manhattan, Fashionhaus is a 3,500-square-foot showroom for a number of European fashion labels. The flexible and open loft environment features custom-designed furniture and display fixtures, including ebonized-maple tables, modular stainless-steel racks, and inset wooden shelving. An undulating, freestanding, wood-slat screen suggests a sense of entry yet maintains the openness and scale of the space. The floor is white poured-resin concrete; on the ceiling, adjustable layered fluorescent strips and spotlights bathe the space in clean, crisp light.

CARRIAGE HOUSE
New York, New York, 2003

Unity and circulation characterize the design of this Greenwich Village home. Originally built as a carriage house for one of the grand nineteenth-century houses on Washington Square, it was converted into a glassblowing studio after 1900. The renovation of the two and a half stories and roof terrace of this landmark building provides a space that facilitates entertaining and also integrates the clients' extensive collection of contemporary art.

Any additions to the building were constrained by New York City's preservation commission, so new spaces including a screening room and wine cellar were constructed by underpinning the structure and excavating a full basement. The open loft composition of the entry floor contains family and dining rooms; the second floor, with its high ceiling and two large windows overlooking the mews, offers a serene environment for the clients' paintings. This space incorporates a skylight installation by James Turrell consisting of colored neon tubes and layers of white scrim. The installation responds to the changing color of the sky, slowly shifting from blue to violet over the course of the day. A switchback staircase made of tinted cast concrete links all levels and the roof terrace. A glass-plank mezzanine stages the lounge area for this rooftop space and also filters natural light into the staircase. The restrained selection of materials – white walls, dark-stained oak floors, and sycamore paneling – underlines the distinctive art and furniture. Rows of bamboo shield rear rooms from the surrounding buildings yet allow daylight to penetrate the interior.

Rich cinnabar red bookcases, redolent of Japanese lacquer boxes of the nineteenth century, are concealed behind buff walnut sliding panels.

NAHA CITY GALLERY AND APARTMENT HOUSE
Naha Fukotoshin, Okinawa, Japan, 2003

The Naha City gallery and apartment house consists of a gallery, jewelry store, three full-floor apartments, and subterranean parking lot. The varied programs are unified by a consistent focus on the interface between interior and exterior. North and south facades sheathe the gallery, retail, and living areas in transparent glass and the bedrooms and bathrooms in opaque glass; the two faces take advantage of the temperate climate of Okinawa, allowing plenty of natural light into the interior. The east and west walls and the floors are cast concrete, durable, affordable, and characteristic of the locale. The solid concrete facades are broken up by small deep windows that look into the stairwell on the east side and the apartment kitchens on the west, creating dramatic lighting effects.

Concrete construction in Okinawa has become particularly refined because the area is subject to both earthquakes and typhoons – a determining factor in the design and material choice of this building. Channels along the edges of the east and west walls and tapered floor slabs evoke a lightweight appearance, expressing an inherent contradiction in the material. On the interior, wood flooring, plaster walls, and built-in wood cabinetry accent the exposed concrete.

Part of an effort by Okinawa prefecture to reclaim
former U.S. military properties, this building is one of
the first in the capital city subject to zoning regulations.
The size and volume are the maximum permitted.

All interior walls and floors are structural. The volume
of the building is constructed of blocks of reinforced
concrete. The exterior face of the concrete is kept
raw and unfinished, while interior surfaces are
finished in glazes of varying degrees of sheen
and tactility.

The layout of the apartments is a hybrid of the Western open loft style and the Japanese room-oriented layout.

146

PERMEABILITY Permeability suggests tha

negotiated, transgressed, and even surpassed.

accepted notions of access. Permeable dem

reestablishing) domain and foster connectior

program, the structural support, the interactic

palette are at once parameters for or, perhaps m

entails a rigorous appraisal of what is dynami

courses of change. Scrutinizing the extent to w

one place and another, between being and sp

of that design, is essential to architecture. Refle

in our time – protean, fragile, and vital – per

many-layered response to an architectural spac

oundaries, both perceived and actual, may be

meability implies access even as it challenges

ations allow flexibility in establishing (and

petween inhabitants and surroundings. The

vith neighbors and surroundings, the material

provocatively, vehicles of permeability. Our work

life and a critical search for resilience amid the

a design establishes communication between

, as well as the parameters and significations

g a distinctly human relationship with the world

ability transcends the pragmatic, soliciting a

WATERMILL HOUSES

Watermill, New York, 2003

This family retreat is comprised of four buildings dispersed across fifteen acres of densely wooded and steeply contoured land in eastern Long Island. The suite includes a three-story main house, single-story guest house, pool house, and workshop / garage.

A contrast to the topographic undulations of the site, the main house is a rational stack of three square boxes: a concrete foundation set into the hilltop; a polyvinyl-screen-wrapped story of bedrooms, slipped from the foundation to create a terrace; and a fully glazed, open-plan "tree house" of living, dining, and generous kitchen. This upper level has views through and across the treetops to the surrounding landscape. An internal court, open to the sky, enhances natural ventilation in the house and provides access to a roof terrace with a more expansive view across the coastal plain, to the shoreline and ocean beyond.

The other structures are equally rational in design and choice of materials. The guest house is a single-story "shoebox." Three sides are full-height glass walls and doors; the fourth, protected by a downward projection of the roof, is seated in a hill. The pool house and pool, cast in concrete, are likewise partially inserted into a hillside. A recreation area at poolside is sheltered under a polyvinyl screen stretched taut over a cantilevered canopy.

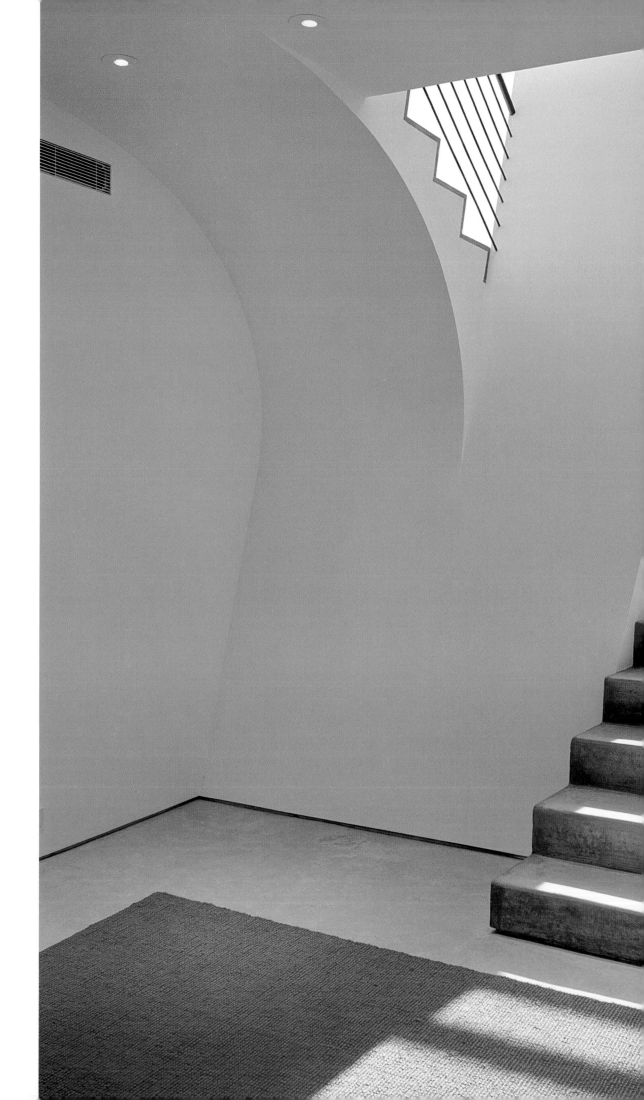

The glass-plank floor of the internal court on the
third floor doubles as a skylight for this porous
transitory space at the center of the second level.
Cantilevered fir steps define the primary interior
stairwell; the vertical circulation area doubles as
a ventilation shaft.

A prefabricated aluminum storefront window system has been adapted for the glass walls and doors of the guest house. Placing the window system in a densely wooded rather than an urban terrain calls into question concepts of intimacy, organic versus synthetic, and permeability.

CORPORATE OFFICE

Fairfield County, Connecticut, 2004

The design of this two-level, twenty-seven-thousand-square-foot office space for an investment firm allows visual communication among employees and encourages direct relationships between traders and analysts. The plan optimizes light and views, providing a self-evident link between interior and exterior. The centrally located trading area is a double-height atrium open to the two floors of offices. A floating steel and glass stair punctuates the atrium beneath a skylight that delivers natural light to the trading stations. The staircase, at once conduit and quasi-sculptural object, is suspended from four points by three-quarter-inch-thick rods; it deploys its weight precisely at key intervals along the span. Full-height glass partitions separate perimeter offices from interior workstations and integrate the surrounding environment.

SOHO RESIDENCE

New York, New York, 2004

Subtle modulations of space and material were deployed to renovate this single floor of a cast-iron building in historic Soho. Meticulously crafted subdivisions create functional areas while preserving the open character of the space. Rooms that demand separation, such as the bathroom, laundry, and storage, are concentrated in the center of the plan; around the perimeter, and enjoying natural light, are the main living spaces, which flow one into another. The materials cast a feeling of warmth: naturally finished end-grain fir for the floors, sculptural beech paneling for interior walls and cabinets, white plaster in enclosed spaces, and a swathe of muted wallpaper in the den. The kitchen and bathroom contribute to the openness of the loft: clutter hides within cabinets and behind work surfaces.

Beech wall paneling, staggered at irregular intervals,
articulates the passageways. Evincing fractal
geometry, the pattern lends depth to the corridors.

FINANCIAL OFFICE

New York, New York, 2005

This office, which comprises seventy thousand square feet on two floors of an office building in midtown Manhattan, is uncharacteristic of a financial firm: with abundant views over Central Park, an absence of private offices, and many conference rooms for focused discussions, it provides a free and open plan that encourages interaction between principals and employees. The design showcases numerous works of contemporary art. A central, self-supporting stair – a weightless juxtaposition of stainless steel, glass, and limestone – challenges the understanding of a conventional staircase. A dynamic pattern of lights and offset panels of perforated metal animates the ceiling of the upper floor. Acoustically, the ceiling localizes sound, allowing for privacy and low-pitched activity in the otherwise open and busy environment.

The staircase connecting the two floors consists of
seventy-two end-supported folded stainless-steel bars,
ranging in length from sixteen to twenty-one feet.

A slender perch overlooking Central Park and the Pulitzer Fountain serves as a dining commons for company employees.

RECOGNITION To recognize is to grasp an ob

A recognizable form invites notice through asso

overarching qualities of a design that trigger s

a work of architecture. An open plan may be rec

a glass house as a viewing device for its surroun

to the viewer and his or her personal history. Th

ture as a transformative agent for a sequential,

Our work aspires to a generosity and universality

This dynamic relationship takes account of in

will incite a positive response; these environm

underscore the conditions that enhance self-re

: or idea with the mind, to learn or to relearn it.

tion, thought, and memory. It is the subtle and

n association – the implied essence or effect of

nized as opportunity, a high ceiling as optimism,

gs. Each of these assessments exists in relation

lurality inherent in recognition reveals architec-

sequential form of recognition: self-recognition.

at allow for infinite instances of self-recognition.

dual sensibilities to create environments that

ts reliably encourage a sense of recognition to

nition.

HOUSE ON THE UPPER EAST SIDE

New York, New York, 2005

This large new house in New York City presents to its neighborhood of early-twentieth-century buildings a crisp modernist face. Clad in large slabs of Wisconsin limestone and resin-backed mahogany and detailed with blackened-steel window casings and an inset entrance, the street front suggests invitation and shelter. The fully glazed piano nobile hangs from the punctuated bulk of the two upper stories.

The clients' communal and entertaining needs are met on the first floor with kitchen, living room, and double dining room. These areas are separated by sliding stainless-steel-mesh acoustical panels. The panels may be banded together to form intimate and discrete areas and to buffer sound; or they may be tucked into a thin wall alcove to provide a generous area with a continuous circulation flow. Similarly, the rear wall of railed glass doors can be opened directly to a courtyard.

In the basement, a large gymnasium / dance studio was carved from bedrock. An exercise room and an arts and crafts workshop, both skylit, also sustain the recreational and cultural activities of the family. The two upper floors are dedicated to private areas.

The stairwell hangs from one of the four walls that surround its faceted form. Natural light from a large skylight above slips sidewise into the space of the stair, swelling in the gaps around the edges of the lower flange of the structure.

PLOTKIN RESIDENCE
New York, New York, 2005

A complete reconstruction and transformation was undertaken for this small historic building in Tribeca, originally constructed in 1919. The glazed terra-cotta exterior cladding, in considerable disrepair, was restored to the standards of the New York City Landmarks Preservation Commission, while the interior was entirely rebuilt into three levels of living space, including a rooftop addition. Expansive windows enhance the perceptual size of the limited interior area, inviting filtered sunlight into the home. The diffuse glow complements a rich selection of wood, stone, and marble. A cantilevered glass staircase barely veiled by a floor-to-ceiling bronze-bar partition ushers light into the core of the residence. Construction of the penthouse involved lowering the existing roof of the main structure to accommodate a warped, luminescent crown. Though the penthouse roof is purely level, walls of high-strength laminated compound-curved glass create a dynamic plan as well as a distorted reflection of the adjacent streetscape.

The top flight of the building's three-level staircase consists of two-inch-thick glass planks cantilevered from three-inch-wide steel clamps welded to an eight-inch steel tube set in a twelve-inch-thick masonry wall. The screen partition is made of thirteen and a half feet of bronze bar.

WEST NINETEENTH STREET CONDOMINIUM

New York, New York, 2006

This new condominium building in West Chelsea will contain twelve floors of apartments, upper-floor terraces, recreation areas, and a courtyard. The street facade is a window wall framed in clear anodized aluminum and bounded by a ribbon of gradated aluminum panels in nine different shades of indigo. The ribbon develops its depth along the southeast-facing lot-line facade, unfolding into a screen of 2,500 panels. Interiors are characterized by wood flooring, laminate cabinetry, and stone countertops.

DRAWINGS

ABELL RESIDENCE
New York, New York, 1998
2,500 square feet

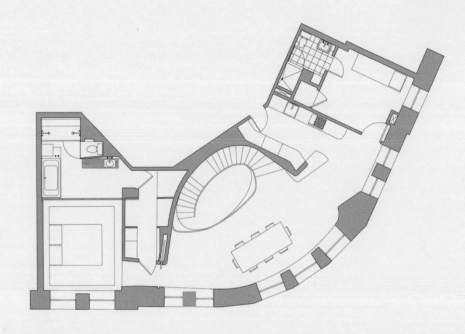

Upper Level Plan

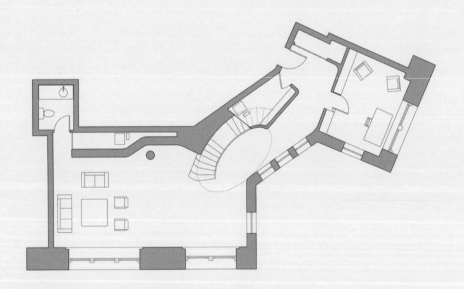

Lower Level Plan

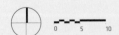

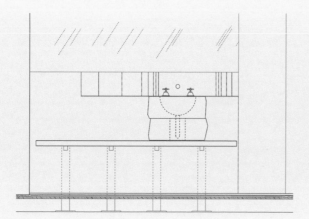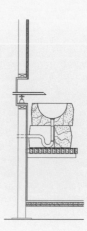

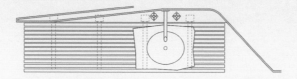

Vanity Elevation, Section, and Plan

Project Managers/Team Leaders: Calvert Wright, Carmen Lenzi
Project Team: Maria Gray, Namrata Gupta, Antonia Kwong,
Pamela Nixon, Douglas Pancoast

LITTLE RED SCHOOL HOUSE AND ELISABETH IRWIN HIGH SCHOOL
New York, New York, 1999, 2002
55,000 square feet

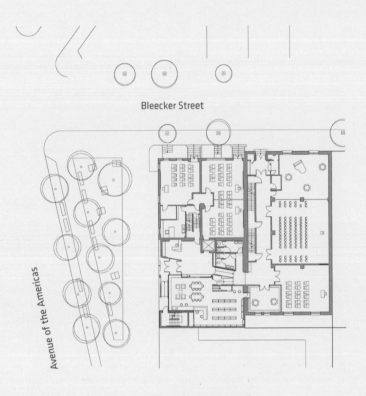

Site/First Floor Plan

Section Looking North

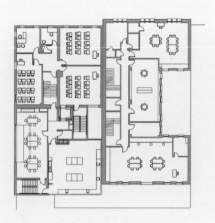

Third Floor Plan

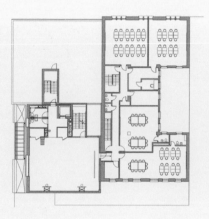

Fourth Floor Plan

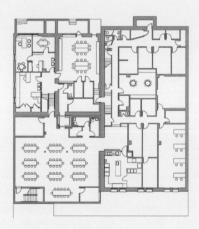

Basement Plan

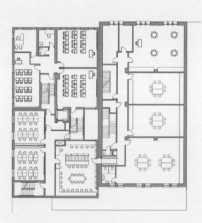

Second Floor Plan

Project Manager/Team Leader: Carmen Lenzi
Project Team: Doris Annen-Feld, Shiben Banerji, Juliana Chittick,
Erica Friedland, Inge Gottschling, Maria Gray, Christine Harper,
Sven Hertel, David Later, Yeekai Lim, Stacy Millman, Kris Mun,
Pamela Nixon, David Robbins, Jorg Schmitt, Douglas Smith,
Kirk Soderstrom, Suzanne Weigele, Bobby Young, Jorge Zapata

MoMA DESIGN STORE, MIDTOWN
New York, New York, 1999
5,000 square feet

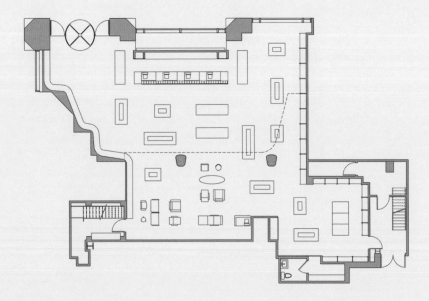

Plan

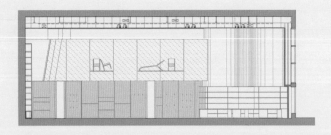

Section Looking South

0   5   10

Project Manager/Team Leader: Ellen Martin
Project Team: Jeff Babienko, Maria Gray, Sherri Harvey,
Thomas Juul-Hansen, John Lashley, Yeekai Lim, Kris Mun

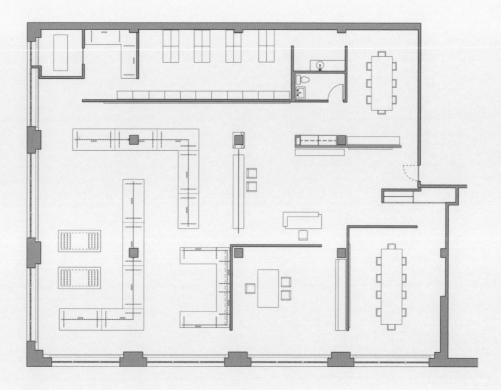

Plan

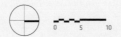

Project Manager/Team Leader: Calvert Wright
Project Team: Jason Foster, Phil Schmerbeck

SHISEIDO STUDIOS
New York, New York, 1999
4,200 square feet

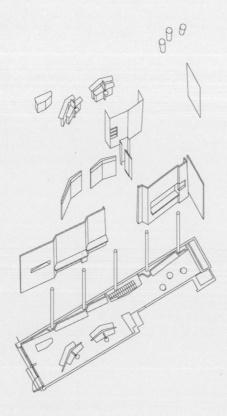

Axonometric

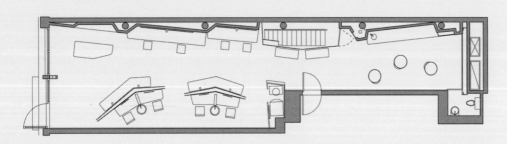

Plan

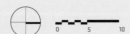

0   5   10

Santa Monica, California, 2000
2,300 square feet

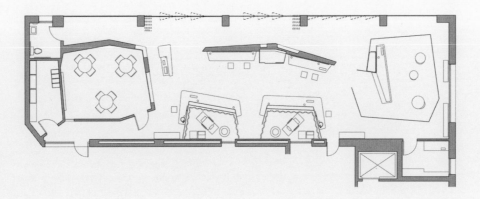

Plan

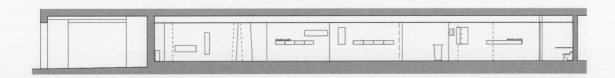

Section Looking East

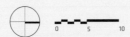

Project Manager/Team Leader: Antonia Kwong
Project Team: Julia Bensieck, Erica Friedland, Yeekai Lim, Selin Maner,
Stacy Millman, Kris Mun, Dorothy Ollesh, Igor Siddiqui, Philip Speranza

217

WEST VILLAGE TOWNHOUSE
New York, New York, 2000
4,000 square feet

Third Floor Plan

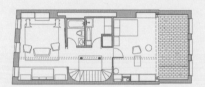

Second Floor Plan

First Floor Plan

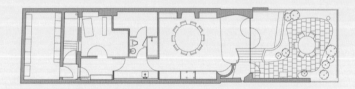

Basement Plan

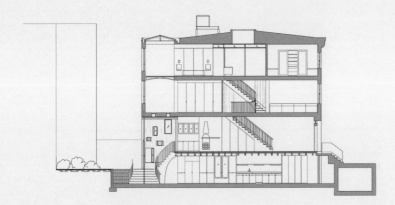

Section Looking South

Project Manager/Team Leader: Christine Harper
Project Team: Antonia Kwong, Edgar Papazian, Philip Speranza

HOLBROOK RESIDENCE
New York, New York, 2000
7,000 square feet

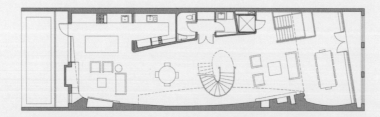

Third Floor Plan

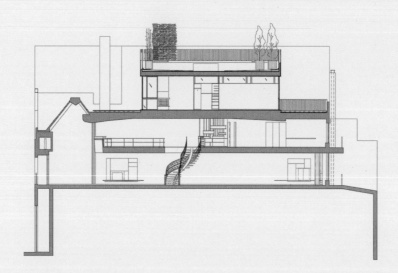

Section Looking West

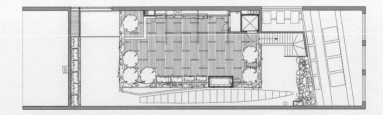

Roof Plan

Penthouse Plan

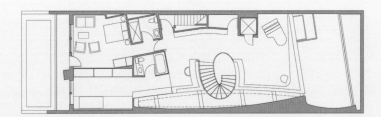

Fourth Floor Plan

Project Managers/Team Leaders: Pamela Nixon, Joanna Chen, Stacy Millman
Project Team: Heather Braun, Juliana Chittick, Namrata Gupta, Jamie Palazzolo

BONNIE'S K9
New York, New York, 2000
1,500 square feet

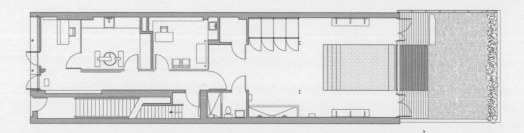

Plan

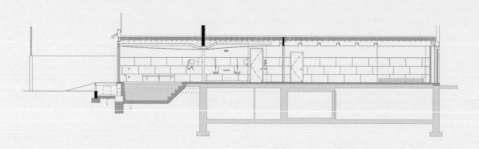

Section Looking South

Project Manager/Team Leader: Carmen Lenzi
Project Team: Yeekai Lim, Igor Siddiqui, Erin Vali

MoMA DESIGN STORE, SOHO
New York, New York, 2001
9,500 square feet

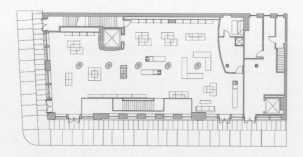

Ground Floor Plan

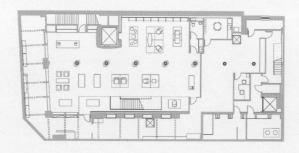

Lower Floor Plan

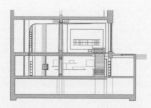

Section Looking North

Project Managers/Team Leaders: Pamela Nixon, Ellen Martin
Project Team: David Later, Jamie Palazzolo, Erin Vali

IRISH HUNGER MEMORIAL
New York, New York, 2002
16,320 square feet

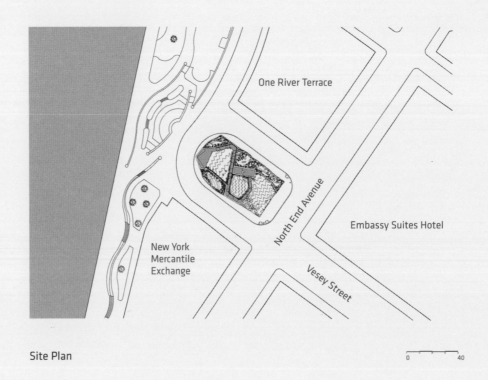

One River Terrace

North End Avenue

Embassy Suites Hotel

New York
Mercantile
Exchange

Vesey Street

Site Plan

0   40

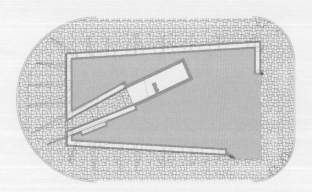

Base and Sidewalk Plan

Upper Level Plan

0   5   10

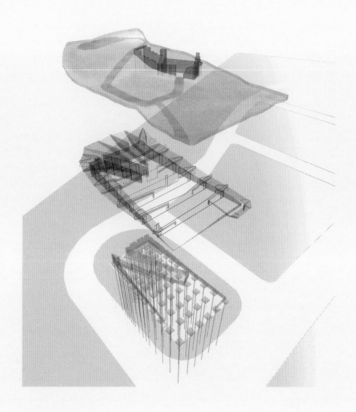

Design Diagram

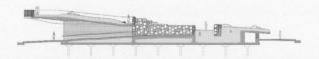

Section

Project Manager/Team Leader: Jeffrey Etelamaki
Project Team: Jeff Babienko, Shiben Banerji, Andreas Benzig,
Raphaelle Golaz, Kristina Hellhake, Sven Hertel, Michael Imranyi, Eun Kim,
Douglas Kocher, Antonia Kwong, Dominique Moret, Jamie Palazzolo,
Erica Skelly, Claudia Wallasch

MANHATTAN DUPLEX
New York, New York, 2002
1,400 square feet

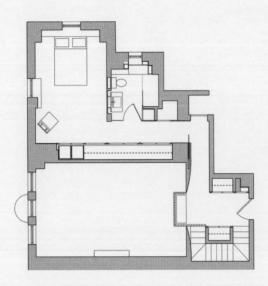

Upper Level Plan

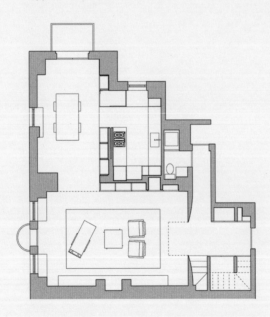

Lower Level Plan

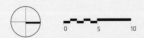

0   5   10

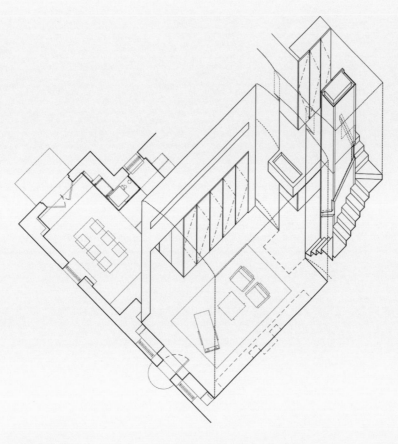

Axonometric

Project Manager/Team Leader: Phil Schmerbeck
Project Team: Joanna Chen, Sven Hertel, Erik Millward, Igor Siddiqui

EAST SIDE PENTHOUSE
New York, New York, 2002
6,500 square feet

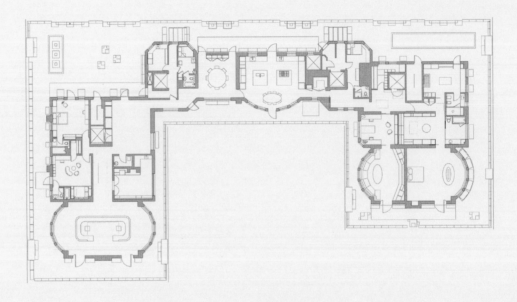

Plan

0 5 10

Project Manager/Team Leader: Christine Harper
Project Team: Joanna Chen, Douglas Kocher, David Later,
Stacy Millman, Morgan Fleming
Interior Design: Tony Ingrao

FASHIONHAUS
New York, New York, 2003
3,500 square feet

Plan

Section Looking West

0   5   10

Project Manager/Team Leader: Antonia Kwong
Project Team: Douglas Smith, Kirk Soderstrom

CARRIAGE HOUSE
New York, New York, 2003
4,200 square feet

Third Floor Plan

Second Floor Plan

Ground Floor Plan

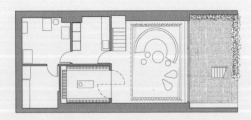

Lower Floor Plan

0   5   10

Section Looking West

Project Managers/Team Leaders: Jeffrey Etelamaki, Igor Siddiqui
Project Team: Michael Imranyi, Ramon Ocampo, Edgar Papazian
Interior Design: India Mahdavi Hudson

NAHA CITY GALLERY AND APARTMENT HOUSE
Naha Fukotoshin, Okinawa, Japan, 2003
6,900 square feet

Second and Third Floor Plan

Fourth Floor Plan

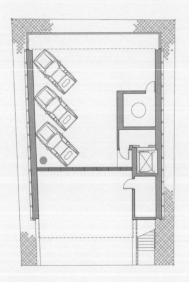

Parking Plan

First Floor Plan

0   5   10

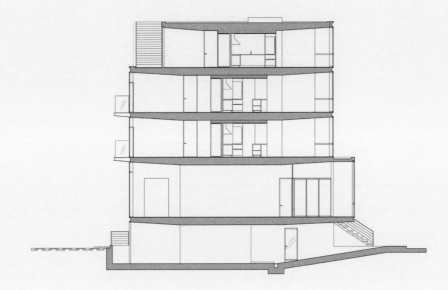

Section Looking East

Project Manager/Team Leader: Joanna Chen
Project Team: Sven Hertel, Erik Millward, Anja Murke,
Christina Schwaegergen, Amy Stein, Jesse Wark, Suzanne Weigele

1. Main House
2. Guest House
3. Pool House
4. Tennis Court
5. Parking

Site Plan

0   40

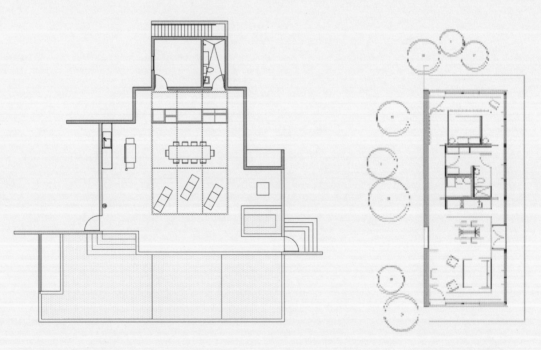

Pool House Plan

Guest House Plan

0   5   10

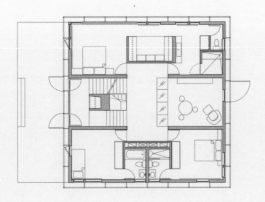

Second Floor Plan

Third Floor Plan

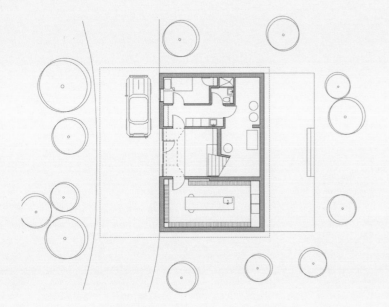

First Floor Plan

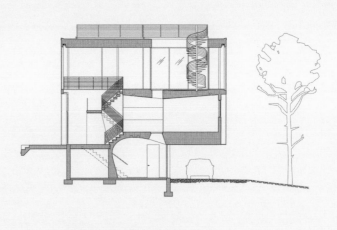

Section Looking South

Project Manager/Team Leader: Carmen Lenzi
Project Team: Joanna Chen, Juliana Chittick, Raphaelle Golaz,
Antonia Kwong, Igor Siddiqui, Erin Vali, Jorge Zapata

Second Floor Plan

First Floor Plan

0   10

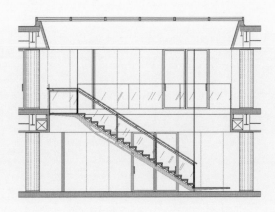
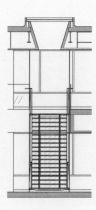

Section Looking West   Section Looking South

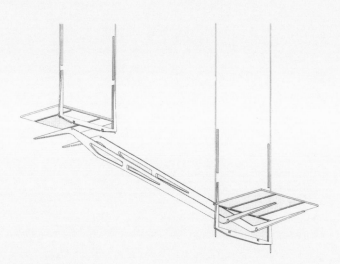

Stair Axonometric

Project Manager/Team Leader: Douglas Kocher
Project Team: Heather Braun, Juliana Chittick, Michael Imranyi,
David Later, Phil Schmerbeck, Jorge Zapata

237

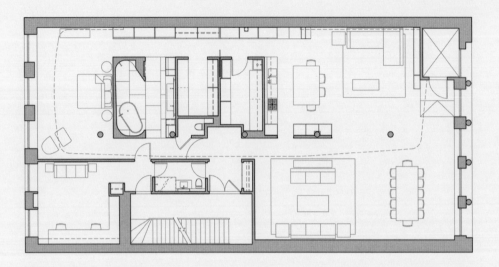

Plan

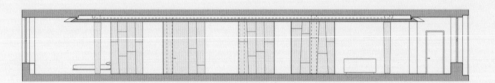

Section Looking North

Project Manager/Team Leader: Ellen Martin
Project Team: Heather Braun, Jesse Wark

238

FINANCIAL OFFICE
New York, New York, 2005
54,000 square feet

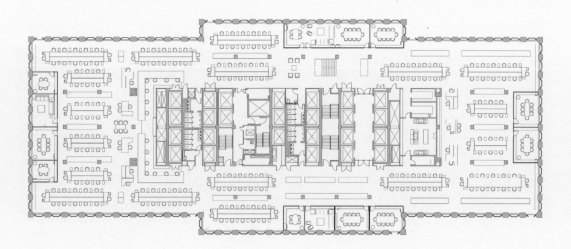

Upper Level Plan

Lower Level Plan

0   10

Project Managers/Team Leaders: Phil Schmerbeck, Mile Verovic
Project Team: Gerald Bodziak, Manon Fantini, Jason Foster, Antonio
Furgiuele, Sebastian Kaempf, Sibylle Kossler, Simon Lee, Texer Nam,
Anke Roogenbuck, Chieko Takahashi
Interior Design: Alexia Kondylis

HOUSE ON THE UPPER EAST SIDE
New York, New York, 2005
14,000 square feet

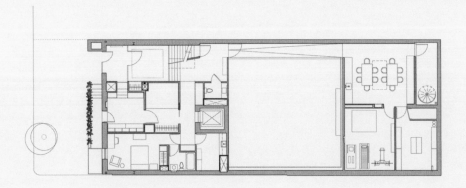

Ground Floor Plan

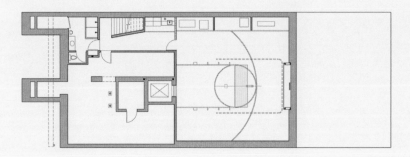

Lower Floor Plan

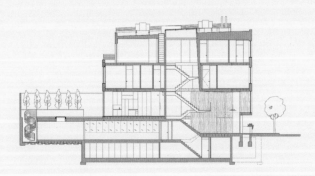

Section Looking East

Fourth Floor Plan

Third Floor Plan

Second Floor Plan

Project Managers/Team Leaders: Christine Harper, Igor Siddiqui
Project Team: Anna Baltschun, Heather Braun, Jinhee Chu, Cedric
Cornu, Jason Foster, Emily Kirkland, Stacey Mariash, Texer Nam,
Anke Roogenbuck, Phil Schmerbeck, Gary Stoltz
Interior Design: with Celeste Cooper

PLOTKIN RESIDENCE
New York, New York, 2005
3,000 square feet

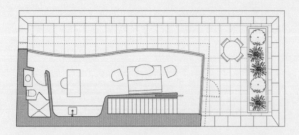

Penthouse Plan

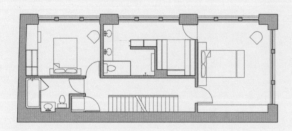

Third Floor Plan

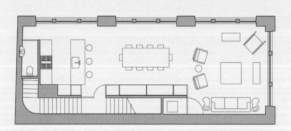

Second Floor Plan

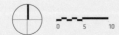

Section Looking East

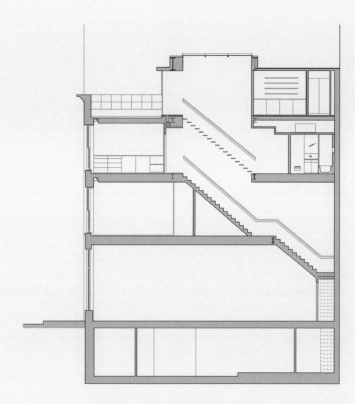

Section Looking South

Project Manager/Team Leader: Ellen Martin
Project Team: Heather Braun, Deborah Fogel, Igor Siddiqui

WEST NINETEENTH STREET CONDOMINIUM
New York, New York, 2006
31,500 square feet

Second Through Eighth Floor Plan

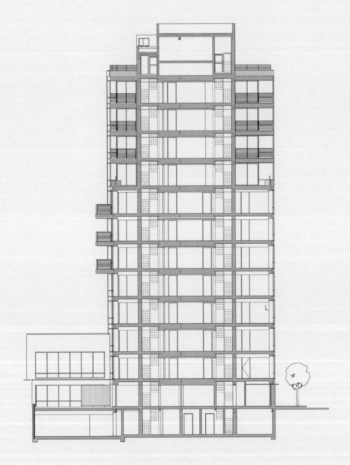

Section Looking East

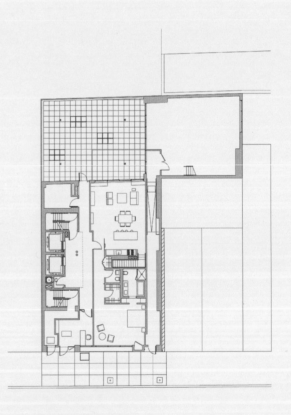

Ground Floor Plan

0   10

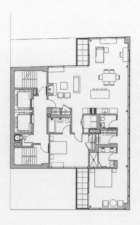

Eleventh Floor Plan

Twelfth Floor Plan

Ninth Floor Plan

Tenth Floor Plan

Project Managers/Team Leaders: Christine Harper, Bo Lee
Project Team: Jack Brough, Gerri Davis, Sebastian Kaempf, Carmen Lenzi,
David Moon, Anke Roogenbuck, Phil Schmerbeck, Igor Siddiqui,
Chieko Takahashi, Aaron Vaden-Youmans

BIOGRAPHIES

David Piscuskas

David Piscuskas, FAIA, is a founding member of 1100 Architect, PC, in New York. He received a bachelor of arts degree from Brown University in 1979. While there, he studied architecture at the Rhode Island School of Design. In 1982, he received a master of architecture degree from the University of California, Los Angeles. Piscuskas is currently a professor of architecture at Parsons The New School for Design in New York.

Juergen Riehm

Juergen Riehm, FAIA, is a founding member of 1100 Architect, PC, in New York. Born and raised in Germany, he received a diploma in architecture from Fachhochschule Rhineland-Pfalz in Trier, Germany, in 1977; in 1982, he received a postgraduate degree in architecture from the Städelschule, Academy of Fine Arts, Frankfurt. Riehm is currently a professor of architecture at Parsons The New School for Design in New York.

1100 Architect

1100 Architect, founded in 1983, is the New York–based architecture studio of David Piscuskas and Juergen Riehm. 1100 was founded on the beliefs that architecture is an important contribution to our society, capable of motivating and inspiring users; that the incorporation into an architectural work of a client's desires is vital to its meaning and distinction; and that architecture is an all-encompassing art form, capable of portraying and transforming all facets of life and nature. 1100 has completed numerous residential, commercial, and institutional projects with careful attention to detail and to the flow of space, producing architecture that is at once serene, purposeful, and playful.

STUDIO TEAM

1998–2006

Our studio teams, past and present, are an essential part of 1100 Architect:

Doris Annen-Feld	Antonio Furgiuele	Noah Levine	Giovanni Santana
Jeff Babienko	Raphaelle Golaz	Yeekai Lim	Sebastian Saure
Anna Baltschun	Jessica Gordon	Stacey MacDiarmid	Marcus Schafer
Shiben Banerji	Liz Grace	Pia Maier-Schriever	Kristina Scheetz
Julia Bensieck	Maria Gray	Selin Maner	Phil Schmerbeck
Andreas Benzig	Dominic Griffin	Stacey Mariash	Jessica Schmidt
Michael Bitterman	Namrata Gupta	Mandi Marsh	Jörg Schmidt
Gerald Bodziak	Ana-Maria Gutierrez	Ellen Martin	Christian Schwab
Heather Braun	Christine Harper	Stacy Millman	Christina Schwaegergen
Jack Brough	Sherri Harvey	Erik Millward	Pia Sebastian
Sinead Burke	Gabriela Hauser	Elaine Monchak	Kimberly Shin
Liz Campbell	Kristina Hellhake	David Moon	Vera Shur
Margaret Carey	Sven Hertel	Dominique Moret	Igor Siddiqui
Jinny Chang	Justine Hsieh	Jamie Mosher	Camilla Skaane
Emily Chang-Zidarov	Katrin Huetz	Kris Mun	Erica Skelly
Sze-Jui Chao	Mia Ihara	Anja Murke	Douglas Smith
Amy Chapman	Michael Imranyi	Texer Nam	Kirk Soderstrom
Joanna Chen	Yunhee Jeong	Magnus Nilsson	Devi Somai
Cristina Chidu	Mairin Jerome	Pamela Nixon	Philip Speranza
Juliana Chittick	Thomas Juul-Hansen	Neda Nohandani	Amy Stein
Kaity Chou	Sebastian Kaempf	Ramon Ocampo	Gary Stoltz
Jinhee Chu	Kristina Kelker	Ringo Offerman	Diana Su
Sookhee Chun	Alessandra Kim	Dorothy Ollesh	Lisa Su
Catherine Clark	Eun Kim	Jamie Palazzolo	Chieko Takahashi
Cedric Cornu	Stephanie King	Douglas Pancoast	Amy Thornton
Gerri Davis	Emily Kirkland	Astrid Pankrath	Llaria Tonetti
Jason Delmotte	Douglas Kocher	Edgar Papazian	Jean-Marie Truchard-Eckert
Danae Dinicola	Marion Kocot	Laura Porter	Tamaki Uchikawa
Melanie Domino	Jennifer Koreckey	Orlando Quarless	Murat Uyanmis
Maria Emminghausen	Sibylle Kossler	Erica Quinones	Aaron Vaden-Youmans
Jeffrey Etelamaki	Antonia Kwong	Abby Rabinowitz	Erin Vali
Harriet Evans	Marie LaFerrara	Siobhan Reagan	Mile Verovic
Manon Fantini	John Lashley	Mark Rintoul	Shivalika Vohra
Morgan Fleming	David Later	David Robbins	Claudia Wallasch
Deborah Fogel	Sarah Lavery	Anke Roogenbuck	Jesse Wark
Matilda Forsberg	Cyrille LeBihan	Liam Ross	Suzanne Weigele
Jason Foster	Bo Lee	Mirko Ruppenstein	Calvert Wright
Patrick Foster	Simon Lee	Patricia Ryan	Bobby Young
Erica Friedland	Carmen Lenzi	Mark Salyer	Jorge Zapata

CONSULTANTS AND ADVISERS

1998–2006

Our work could not be achieved without the professionals, engineers, architects, and designers who have assisted us with expert advice, ideas, and experience:

Chris Agostino
Dominick Agostino
Chris Anderson
Robert Anderson
Ross Anderson
Bill Andresen
Pat Arnett
Jay Asheton-Langdon
Michael Astram
Paul Austi
Arpad Baksa
Salvatore Barbieri
Wilson Bassey
Andrew Bast
Ira Beer
Israel Berger
Steve Bienkowski
Susan Bilenker
Laszlo Bodak
Martin Bowen
Alfred Brand
Serge Budzyn
Vincent Byrne
Walter Firestone Chatham
Henlia Chen
Masaharu China
Peter Christensen
Kam Chui
John Clancy
David Clark
Michele Clement
Geoffrey Cook
Celeste Cooper
Nino D'Antonio
Steven D'Antonio

Russell Davies
Carmen DeVito
Eric Fischl
Tom Fisher
John Fox
Belmont Freeman
Nina Freudenberger
Robert Friedland
Michael Gabellini
Melbourne Garber
Robert F. Gatje
Dean Gaules
Ralph Gentile
Gerry George
John Giannetti
Richard Gluckman
Paul Goldberger
April Gornik
Christopher Hager
Reginald Hough
Tony Ingrao
Michael Ishler
Natasha Jen
Dimitri Jeurissen
Kristen Johnson
Wendy Evans Joseph
Metin Karacas
Moshe Kasman
Randy Kemper
Robert Klotzbach
Alexia Kondylis
George Langer
Hyung Lee
David Lewis
Bruce Lilker

India Mahdavi
Douglas Mass
Kenneth McComb
John McKeough
Kit Middleton
Roger Miller
Denis Milsom
Neil Moiseev
Kent Nash
Signe Nielson
Richard M. Olcott
Nat Oppenheimer
Robin Osler
Alfred Pang
Elizabeth Peterson
Giuseppe Pica
Greg Pillori
Aaron Pine
Rocco Piscatello
Carmine Pizzo
Alan Poeppel
Miguel Pons
Kurt Ricci
David Rossini
John Ryan
Joseph Sage
George Schell
Christopher Scholz
Frank Schuck
Andrea Schwan
Bill Schwinghammer
Boris Shpilberg
Lee H. Skolnick
Richard Souto
Hiroko Sueyoshi

Brian Tolle
James Turrell
Lisa Westheimer
Peter Wheelwright
Tod Williams
Gail Eileen Wittwer
Soo Wong Lee
Philip Yee
Zack Zanolli
Martin Zubatkin

BUILDERS AND ARTISANS

1998–2006

We consistently learn a great deal from the builders, craftspeople, and others who share their knowledge
and their dedication to the highest level of construction and craftsmanship:

Karen Atta
Gadi Benyaacov
George Bishop
Bruce Bjork
Robert Blanda
Susan Blum
Alan Bouknight
Mary Bright
Joe Bruno
Bob Bruskin
Bob Buskin
Renato Busljeta
Eliot Cabot
Saskia Cacanindin
Joseph Carione
Anthony Carvette
Frank Cashin
Edward Colbert
Peter Costello
John Couch
Steven Cozzolino
Tim Crowley
Paul Deutsch
Steven Diblozio
David Doernberg
Johnny Donadic
Steve Donadic
Galin Dutter
Gene Dwarkin
David Esbin
Tammy Espaillat-Bautista
Greg Fergeuson
Steve Ferraro
Steve Fetner
John Fogler

Peter Folsom
Vinnie Galiano
Arthur Gilman
Karen Gilman
Bruce Gitlin
James Gladysz
David Greenberg
Steve Hass
Julie Hatfield
Ed Hennessy
Charles Hickok
Andy Hoffman
Eric Hoffman
Steve Hogden
John Hosford
Evan Hughes
Tim Hupfer
Jim Hurley
Brian Jevremov
Nick Jordache
David Keane
David Kelleran
John Kern
Ray Kilroy
Larry King
Peter Kirkileas
Gerry Klinger
Chris Krukowski
Suzy Kunz
Steven Lamazor
Peter Latek
Michael LaPenna
Kurt Lebeck
Jeremy Lebensohn
Jerry Lefteratos

Joe Leonard
Lennie Leone
Michael Leone
Anthony Lepore
Ron Lessard
Stuart Liben
Stuart Liebman
Dennis Lin
Dennis Loebs
Derek Loehmer
Joe Marques
Glenn Mazzeo
Enda McIntyre
Chris McNally
Mike Melanophy
Philip Meskin
Lee Miller
Roger Miller
Richard Moon
Steve Musto
Patrick Nash
Paul O'Donoghue
Willie Opalka
Mike Payne
Paul Pianpiano
Jim Pieper
Larry Platman
Joseph Pocognamo
Jeff Pond
Carlos Queiroz
Doug Rice
Randy Rollner
Gary Romanovicz
John Schaub
Anthony Scorcia

Robert Scott
Peter Sheridan
Aidan Shevlin
Emmanuel Skountzos
Alex Smartenko
Tom Smith
Stan Snyder
Ruben Suare
Donald Sussman
Peter Thaler
Katsuko Tokuchi
Steve Urbatsch
Roman Uszynski
Nick Villani
Ted Vitale
Peter Vuletic
Philip Vuletic
Russ Wadhams
Stacey Waggoner
Beriah Wall
James Wong
Ken Wright

ACKNOWLEDGMENTS

We thank our publisher, Gianfranco Monacelli, and The Monacelli Press for sustained interest in our work and ongoing attention to architecture and design. Andrea Monfried, our editor at Monacelli, contributed her talents and insights to this publication. Abbott Miller and Christine Moog of Pentagram brought an elegant, beautiful vision to the design of the book. Their assiduous collaboration and cogent realization of our ideas are invaluable. Donald Albrecht's perceptive essay introduces this volume, and we are grateful for his observations. We acknowledge photographers Peter Aaron and Michael Moran, who are responsible for most of the images in this book. Their vision and clarity in representing our work is greatly appreciated. We are especially grateful to Laura Porter, a vital participant in the making of this book. She contributed to and refined all aspects of the text and worked with steady, tireless proficiency toward its completion. Maria Emminghausen, Melanie Domino, and Matilda Forsberg from our office provided important support in developing the material.

We appreciate that our profession allows us to collaborate with people of talent and wisdom. Ines Elskop, former partner and longtime friend, has been an invaluable influence in our careers and lives; her loyalty, guidance, and provocative insights are a source of encouragement and inspiration. We are grateful to Ines for moderating the dialogue published here. Andrea Schwan brings important advice, clarity, and scope to the breadth of our work. Her energy and wisdom are sincerely valued. We also thank Jack Van Horne, Mitch Koshers, and Jerome Wile for their advice and support of all aspects of our professional practice. Peter Wheelwright, David Lewis, and Paul Goldberger are respected colleagues who have supported and inspired our teaching for many years. We thank them for their trust in our ideas.

The work in this volume would not be complete were it not for the persistent efforts and talents of the builders, engineers, and colleagues with whom we have collaborated over the past twenty-three years. Nino D'Antonio brings ingenuity and enthusiasm to every project, and Nat Oppenheimer, with whom we have taught and collaborated, has our respect and gratitude. Due immeasurable thanks is our staff of architects, associates, and assistants, past and present, who have shared with us their talents, ideas, and extraordinary work. In particular, Christine Harper, Carmen Lenzi, Ellen Martin, Phil Schmerbeck, and Douglas Kocher deserve recognition for their fine work and commitment to 1100 Architect. Finally, we thank our clients, who are inextricably linked to our work; their challenges and support have helped hone our best projects.

The support and wisdom of our family, friends, and children have made this book possible.

PHOTOGRAPHY CREDITS

Peter Aaron, ESTO
40–41, 65, 66, 67, 69, 73, 77, 78, 80, 81, 82–83, 87, 88, 90, 91, 92–93, 95, 98–99, 100–101, 102, 103, 105, 106, 107, 108, 109, 110, 111, 112–13, 117, 118, 119, 120–21, 122–23, 124–25, 131, 132–33, 134–35, 136–37, 151, 152–53, 154, 155, 156–57, 158–59, 160–61, 162–63, 164–65, 166–67, 169, 170–71, 173, 176–77, 181, 182–83, 184–85, 186–87

Tom Bonner
60, 61, 62–63

Peter Mauss, ESTO
97

Michael Moran
23, 25, 26–27, 28, 29, 31, 32–33, 34–35, 36, 37, 38–39, 42–43, 52–53, 54–55, 68, 70–71, 74–75, 76, 127, 128–29, 172, 174–75, 189, 190, 191, 192–93, 194, 195, 196–97, 199, 200, 201, 202, 203, 204, 205

Shinichi Sato
138–39, 140, 142, 143, 144–45, 146–47

Paul Warchol
44–45, 47, 48–49, 50–51, 59